MEUSES, CODES, AND REALMS

Joelle Margarete

A publication of

Eber & Wein Publishing

Pennsylvania

Meuses, Codes, and Realms

Copyright © 2024 by Joelle Margarete

Library of Congress
Cataloging in Publication Data

ISBN 978-1-60880-766-6

Proudly manufactured in the United States of America by

Eber & Wein Publishing

Pennsylvania

Dedication

I dedicate this book to a number of people, as every one of them has contributed to it. My home state, New Jersey, is the biggest reason that I am who I am. There are two poems about New Jersey in this collection: New Jersey Crossroads Of The Revolution and Silent Movies. All of the cats that I have been blessed to live with have been my furry meuses. As I look through their eyes, I see the world in a new and wonderous way. My mother has encouraged my writing, so thanks to her. My Husband has been a loyal supporter, so credit to him, as well. He is the codes part of the title, as he is in construction. The two school newspapers, and the school magazine, were great writing experiences. The teacher advisors were big supporters of their student writers. My Navy shipmates helped me to learn the discipline and dedication every writer needs. A few other special groups that I need to mention are U S veterans of all services as we share a special veteran's bond. I dedicate this book to all of the past and future veterans that are part of the "22 a day "crisis. If anyone has lost a loved one to suicide, I am right there with you. For every Mental Health Professional that has ever helped me, thank you. Rachel is a shining example of a Mental Health Professional, so a special thank you to her. The realm of the title is the spirit realm. As I have abilities, I deal with two realms, so for others with abilities, I dedicate this book to you. I dedicate this book to everyone at Eber & Wein for encouraging me to publish this book.

CONTENTS

DEDICATION

This poem is dedicated to my late father-in-law. I wrote it the first time he was ill, as there was a chance that he might die. The subject of death was all around me, so I decided to write about it. This poem is a true representation of my thoughts on the subject of death. Even though we take the final walk alone, I do not believe that the people that we love ever truly leave us. They go on to the next realm where they are always close by.

THE LONG WALK

In each life there is one walk always taken alone.

The shadow of our life will leave this world for another.

As our loved ones grieve we will be soaring on angel wings to another plane of existence.

There will be no way to know how or what this walk is like until we take it.

Of all wonder science may study, this is the one it can not.

No one can take this walk for us—this we must do alone.

Fear not the walk, as it is the start of a new existence.

Joelle Margarete

DEDICATION

This poem is dedicated to all of the very special feline fur-balls that left pawprints across my heart. Someday, I will cross the Rainbow Bridge, and see all of you again.

PAWPRINTS BRANDED ON MY HEART

I miss your meows to get my attention.

I miss the way you used to purr when I would pet you.

I miss being able to give you chin rubs.

I miss watching your ears move independently like radar dishes.

I miss feeling your fur rubbing against my legs.

I miss your blank detached brain looks when you were in trouble.

I miss being kneaded by you when you were content.

I miss looking at your beautiful coat.

I miss the way you marked everything with your scent.

I miss being owned by you.

Joelle Margarete

A FELINE'S CURIOSTY ABOUT THE QUARANTINE

What exactly does "quarantine" mean?

Why do the humans work from home?

Why do they stay in pajamas all day?

What are those coverings they put over their faces?

Where are the fun store bags to play in?

Why are they obsessed with toilet paper?

Why are we watching this show again?

Why did our humans start having dinner delivered?

Why do our humans love their hobbies so much, now?

Why does the news make our humans so sad?

Joelle Margarete

A FELINES 12 DAYS OF CATMAS

Day one my human presents to me a fully decorated and lighted Christmas Tree!

Day two my human presents to me two advent calendars filled with toys and treats!

Day three my human presents to me three cat trees for climbing joy!

Day four my human presents to me four catnip socks with organic catnip!

Day five my human presents to me five fish shaped cat toys to attack!

Day six my human presents to me six plastic balls with loud bells inside!

Day seven my human presents to me seven colourful felt mice to bat around!

Day eight my human presents to me eight cat condos for cat napping!

Day nine my human presents to me nine cans of food to savor!

Day ten my human presents to me ten wand toys requiring human power!

Day eleven my human presents to me eleven device toys for charging!

Day twelve my human presents to me twelve bags of treasured treats!

Joelle Margarete

A FELINE'S CARDBOARD TREASURE CHEST

Oh what, oh what are you?

A treasure created out of cardboard just for me!

Shall I fit inside this plaything?

There is but one way to know.

A regal jump will tell me so.

My treasure chest is quite comfortable to be in.

Shall I catnap or lie in wait for my prey to come.

No, no, no I will not share with you.

It is mine, all mine.

Leave me now, to enjoy my treasure chest.

Joelle Margarete

MAJESTIC FELINES

They come in a rainbow of shapes and sizes.

Their graceful stretches are like a ballerina's.

Meow is the only word they speak–but it has endless meanings.

With every part of their body they communicate.

A patch of lazy sunlight causes them to magically appear.

They are as mysterious as the full moon.

Catnip turns them into tiny kittens again.

A finer companion you will never find.

Dimly lit spaces make their eyes all, aglow.

Upon your bed they will take their naps.

Rarely does a cat need a bath.

Their purrs will warm your heart.

Sandpapery kisses they will give you.

A feline is one of God's most magnificent creatures.

Joelle Margarete

KITTENS

They come in an assortment of colours and sizes.

They chase bitzy balls.

They smack at your feet when you move them under the covers.

They put everything in their mouths.

They crawl in your lap for love.

They wrestle with their siblings.

They are always hungry.

They pounce on mousees.

Birds and Humming Birds fascinate them.

They run through the house for no reason.

They are cats in training.

Joelle Margarete

AUGUST

Named for a Roman Caesar.

It's name means inspiring awe.

It is the eight month of the Julian calendar year.

Peridot is its birthstone.

Poppy is the flower of the month.

Leo's and Virgo's abound in this month.

It is the most popular month for birthdays.

The only month with no major holidays in it.

Mirth and laziness thrive as summer freedom slowly draws to a close.

Joelle Margarete

BIRTHDAYS

Colourful cakes.

Brightly wrapped presents.

Off key serenading.

Humorous greeting cards.

Bounce houses.

Silly party games.

Party favours as souvenirs.

Candles to blow out.

Special wishes to be made.

Joelle Margarete

CLOCKS

They come in a variety of styles.

Sizes differ considerably.

One can represent an anniversary or milestone.

Batteries may be required to make them function.

Chimes, bongs, and whistles are heard from many.

A town or city may use one as a local landmark.

Books, and movies often use them as centerpieces.

They help to organize people's lives.

Clocks are objects used by people everyday.

Joelle Margarete

GARDENS

They worship the sun.

Water makes them grow.

The wind makes them dance.

Colourful flowers rule some.

Nourishing vegetables can be produced in them.

Working in them can provide relaxation.

Butterflies visit them.

Joelle Margarete

DEITIES OF THE ANCIENT EGYPTIANS

Over two-thousand of them roamed in Ancient Egypt.

Appearing in the form of animals.

Strange and mysterious creatures with human bodies, and animal heads.

Felines filled their temples with beautiful mews and purrs.

They often chose white as their colour of choice.

Clad in the dress of the socially elite.

Displayed atop their head were resplendent crowns.

In one hand a Ankh-sign, and a scepter in the other.

They ruled the land of Ancient Egypt through legends and myths.

Joelle Margarete

AMERICAN ICONS

A tea soaked harbor.

The Swamp Fox and rebel warfare tactics.

No quarter given to pirates.

The two tragic phantoms at Ford's Theatre.

Cameras to record life's events.

Nickelodeons and the Jersey Shore.

Motels for the horseless carriage devotees.

The Golden Gate Bridge.

American Football.

Comic books and superheroes.

Personal computers as a portal to the world.

Internet animal stars.

Joelle Margarete

DRAGOUNS

Myths of this legendary beast abound through every age and place of mankind.

Grand tales of vast dragon hoards hidden in dark liars surround their existence.

Mere hatchlings at birth they mature into beasts of epic proportions.

Upon land, sea, or air colour changing abilities protect their lives.

Their brilliant, multi-hued teardrop shaped scales protect all but a soft under belly.

Majestic wings set them apart from all other animals.

Deadly breath of fire, ice, or acid crush their foes.

In flight they twist and turn in the most amazing ways.

Using a person's own fear against them is their most fatal weapon.

Forever shrouded in mystery and shadows drakes will live forever.

Joelle Margarete

MOONLIGHT

A vampires delight.

It casts eerie shadows.

Lovers adore it.

Concealment is easy in it.

Evil deeds occur in it.

Ghost ships are seen in it.

Specters appear in it

The world is hidden by it.

Joelle Margarete

FOG

It comes in on cat's feet.

Scandalous secrets are concealed within it.

It is a backdrop for horror movies.

It is attracted to wharfs and seaports.

You can move through it unseen.

In Holmes' world it is eerie.

San Francisco is famous for it.

Joelle Margarete

EARTH BOUND SPIRITS

They are caught between two planes of existence.

Revel themselves in many mysterious ways.

Often appear in the evening hours.

Create a drop in temperature.

Their motives to communicate are varied.

Do not always realize they are the dearly departed.

Stay true to who they were in life.

Are supernatural reminders of terrorist attacks.

May be seeking forgiveness that, sadly, will never come.

Are rarely visible for more than a moment.

At times they foretell of danger.

May not be human, at all.

They fascinate society in every possible way.

Joelle Margarete

JACK'S FOOLISH FIRE

An American vegetable carved into an assortment of looks.

A tribute to a lost soul named Jack.

Based upon the mysterious lights of ignis fatuus.

Their relations are called bogies and punkies.

A simple candle's flame brings them to life.

A truly welcoming beacon to trick or treaters.

They inspired unique carving tools.

Create a truly unusual one and you may win a prize.

A plastic copy often holds a tiny tots candy treasure trove.

Truly the centerpiece of Autumn's first major holiday.

Joelle Margarete

LEGENDS OF THE HEAVENS

Ursa Major and Ursa Minor are the bears of the heavens.

Taurus is the raging white bull of the heavens.

Gemini devoted twin brothers of the heavens.

Perseus and Andromeda eternal lovers in the heavens.

Pisces the fish forever bound together in the heavens.

Leo the famous feline of the heavens.

Draco's reward for loyal service to Juno was immortality in the heavens.

Atlas damned to suffer the burden of the world upon his shoulders evermore.

Joelle Margarete

MOUSE, ZAKARY MOUSE

I extend my paw to greet you.

A beautiful Bombay kitten mix, am I.

Catnip toys if you please.

A cat treat would most welcome.

I only have kisses for my favourite people.

Soaking up the rays is how I like to spend my days.

At night a lap is fine for snuggling.

A better brother will never be found.

My white fur sprinkles make me special.

There is but one Mouse, Zakary Mouse.

Joelle Margarete

NEW JERSEY: CROSSROADS OF THE REVOLUTION

The third state of the Union.

It is the garden state.

Setting of the Battle of Monmouth with it's famous heroine Molly (Hayes) Pitcher.

Land of the Nanticoke Lenni-Lenape Indians.

Home to The Pine Barrons, and Mrs. Leeds thirteenth child.

The state that lights Lady Liberty's torch.

Historic light houses with their still sea watching spirits.

Redecorated by mighty hurricanes each season.

Joelle Margarete

FURRY FELINE NURSES

A variety of colours, and breeds are to be found.

They will lay their paws on you to heal you.

Their soft purrs will help you to rest.

As you sleep, they will watch over you.

When you are cold, they will warm you with their soft warm fur.

They will wait at the door to go to the doctor's with you.

A nurse cat is always on duty, and ready to minister to you.

Joelle Margarete

PROMETHEUS

His name means forethought

Formally a warrior for Zeus.

He favoured primitive man with many gifts.

The greatest gift of all was fire.

The glorious blaze that started man on a new path of brilliance.

Angered by the priceless gift Zeus punished Prometheus.

He was shackled to a cliff and doomed to be torn apart daily by an eagle.

Only to be healed each night so the torture could prolong in the dawn.

His punishment was destined to be eternal.

At long last a kind act of many preceding years ceased his agony to end.

Joelle Margarete

SEASONS

They determine the pace of life.

Require Mother Nature to change her appearance.

Produce crops of assorted varieties.

Change the apparel of folks.

Cause felines to shed their fur.

Offer different religious ceremonies.

Are seen by the changes in sports participated in.

Joelle Margarete

AUTUMN

The soft rustling of brightly coloured leaves in the wind.

The sound of trick or treaters at your door.

Felines curling up on your fleece blankets at night.

Thanksgiving turkey roasting in the oven.

Warm family gatherings at high school football games.

Hot apple cider to warm the spirit.

A crisp evening breeze across your cheek.

The transition time between summer and winter.

Joelle Margarete

SILENT MOVIES

The Keystone Cops.

Film pioneer Max Senate.

Peril far and wide.

Delights aplenty.

Dashing heroes to the rescue.

Stunning damsels to behold.

Hazardous railroad tracks.

Creator of the first movie stars.

Nickelodeons.

Originated in New Jersey.

Joelle Margarete

SNOWMEN

They come in many varieties.

Coal eyes, carrot noses, and sticks for arms are quite common.

A scarf is a common accessory.

Fields of snowy white are their homes.

Countless hours of family fun go into constructing them.

They are a time honoured winter tradition.

Joelle Margarete

THE WORLD OF BOOKS

Tales of the macabre will terrify you.

A mystery will challenge your mind.

New foods appear in your days through cookbooks.

A biography brings your heroes to life.

Science fiction stories transport your mind to new universes.

Narratives of suspense leave you on the edge of your seat.

A romantic saga can make your heart sing.

Your inner swashbuckler is released in an adventure chronicle.

Legends of antiquity spring to life from history books.

Children go off to dreamland with fairy tales.

A book transports you to many new worlds.

Joelle Margarete

SUPER HEROS

They dress in costumes to conceal their "true" identities.

Some have spectacular super powers, or lists to follow.

Often times, they are wealthy, public figures.

Their super hero names declare something about them.

Behind the scenes there is often a team supporting them.

Their high tech gadgets, and secret lairs are valuable to them.

Righting wrongs, and dispensing justice are their lofty goals.

Some people dread them; while others are in awe of them.

The cities that they protect require them.

Books, and movies follow their numerous adventures.

Joelle Margarete

A VISIT TO THE BEACH

Warm sand between your toes.

Wearing fashionable swimwear.

Sizzling summer books to devour.

Bonfires to gather around.

Creating grand sand castles.

Swimming in the ocean.

Viewing fireworks in the sky.

Collecting seashells in a bucket.

Joelle Margarete

WIND

It turns colourful pinwheels.

It cools down summer heat.

It can destroy at high speeds.

It is a source of energy.

It feels cool against your face.

It cannot truly be seen.

Joelle Margarete

THE NEW CROCKERY

Oh, how wonderful, the new crockery has arrived!

How lovely and pristine the pieces are.

There are no chips, and they are as bright as can be.

Still, as we give the previous set away, I feel a bit forlorn.

The previous set holds so many precious memories.

They were my first set of matching dishes.

I was so proud to serve the first meal on them.

There were so many special occasions that they graced my table.

Through countless meals they did their silent duty.

It is my fondest wish that the new owners appreciate them, as I have.

Joelle Margarete

HEROS OF THE UNION

Firefighters that battle the eternal flames.

Police officers that enforce our country's laws.

Suffragettes that gave women the right to vote.

Professors that educate future generations.

Veterinarians that keep beloved pets in good health.

Writers that chronicle the history of our times.

Environmentalists that preserve the world we live in.

Service members that spend holidays away from home to keep our freedom, everlasting.

Joelle Margarete

THE CIRCUS EXPERIENCE

The ringmaster appears to hold sway over all.

Cossacks dance in ancient custom.

Clowns appear in tiny cars with pies to throw.

A human cannon ball catapults across the air.

Elephants, Lions, and Tigers do remarkable feats.

Trapeze artists dazzle on the high wire.

Strongmen lift startling quantities of mass.

A sensation of amazement floods you as you observe.

The circus experience draws out the child in us all.

Joelle Margarete

THE SLEEPY LITTLE TOM KITTEN

The sleepy little tom kitten struggles to stay awake.

There are so many delightful things still to do.

So many wonderful toys and yet so little time.

He runs in circles as he fights sleep.

The humans say that a short nap would not harm him.

They do not understand what he will miss if he naps.

Finally, he can keep his eyes open no more.

Sleep overtakes him in spite of his valiant efforts to defeat it.

As he drifts off to dreamland, the humans know that he will soon be awake.

Joelle Margarete

GOOD LUCK CHARMS

A certain number to arrange your life by.

A favourite piece of clothing that always brings a windfall.

Specific cat breeds often bring good fortune to their companions.

Good Trolls with their wild, wild hair will improve your providence.

A shooting star to make all of your wishes come true.

Elephants with their trunks held aloft to bring prosperity.

Horseshoes turned upward to ensure an abundance of blessings.

A special coin to guarantee success.

Good Luck Charms are mementos to be cherished.

Joelle Margarete

OUR SILLY LITTLE BUG

Come quickly, and see what the kitten has discovered!

You sigh and say, girls and their silly little bugs.

Surprise-it is green, huge, and strange looking.

We have NEVER seen its kind before.

Our tortie would save us if she could but reach it.

It hovers in the uppermost corner of the doorway.

Wisely, it remains out of reach of all.

Free my home of this monster the kitten pleads.

Half a can of insect repellent stuns the fiend.

As it drops to the floor, it's wings yet stir.

Actual stomping on it is required to subdue it.

Finally, it may be dropped outside the door.

The kitten now feels safe.

Off to bed with her humans.

Joelle Margarete

OH WESTERN SCRUB-JAY

Majestic jay that favours California's Central Valley.

How beautiful is the blue of your feathers in the golden sunlight.

Your wondrous song fills the air with joy.

To obtain the prize within you break your sunflower seeds on my garden rocks.

Skillfully you sharpen your beak on my redwood fence.

The slyest of thieves of others secret acorn caches.

How charming you look as your cleanse yourself in my birdbath.

May you visit my yard evermore.

Joelle Margarete

ABOUT THE AUTHOR

I was born and raised in New Jersey. I went to U S Navy boot camp after I graduated high school. I am a Cold War veteran and my proudest achievement is helping to bring down The Berlin Wall. I have been writing in different ways most of my life. I worked on two school newspapers, junior high and high school. I worked on the high school magazine, as well. I attended college, but did not graduate. I do value the experience. I live in Northern California with my husband and my cats. My cats are my furry meuses. As I see the world through their eyes, it is a wondrous place full of treasures to be explored. I try to use this unique perspective when I write. My goal is to inspire everyone, kind enough to read my, work, to consider their own thoughts on the subject. I like to read, do crafting, word and other types of puzzles, study history, listen to music and spend time with my kitties.

www.ingramcontent.com/pod-product-compliance
Lightning Source LLC
LaVergne TN
LVHW091321080426

835510LV00007B/596